This journal is in memory of

_____

written with love by

_____

25 24 23 22 21 20   2 3 4 5 6 7 8

ISBN: 978157819

Library of Congress Cataloging-in-Publication Data
  Names: Rowland, Joanna, author. | Baker, Thea, illustrator.
Title: The memory book : a grief journal for children and families /
  written by Joanna Rowland ; illustrated by Thea Baker.
Description: Minneapolis, MN : Beaming Books, 2020. | Audience: Ages 4-8 |
  Summary: "I will always remember you . . .Joanna Rowland's best-selling

  The Memory Box: A Book about Grief has helped thousands of children and families work through the
complex emotions that arise after the loss of a loved one. Now, with The Memory Book, Rowland has
created a beautiful grief journal to help readers put her methods into practice. The Memory Book helps
grieving families process their emotions together by remembering their lost loved one and creating their
own memory album full of photos and keepsakes of the person they lost. With gentle prompts and ideas
for journaling, drawing, and talking through grief, this journal will bring comfort in the midst of loss
and be a keepsake for families for years to come"-- Provided by publisher.
Identifiers: LCCN 2019036352 | ISBN 9781506457819 (hardcover)
Subjects: LCSH: Grief--Juvenile literature. | Death--Juvenile literature.
Classification: LCC BF575.G7 R695 2020 | DDC 155.9/37--dc23
LC record available at https://lccn.loc.gov/2019036352
Control Number: 2019036352

VN0004589; 9781506457819; NOV2020

Beaming Books
510 Marquette Avenue
Minneapolis, MN 55402
Beamingbooks.com

The Memory Book

A Grief Journal for Children and Families

by Joanna Rowland

illustrated by Thea Baker

beaming books
MINNEAPOLIS

Contents

How to use this memory journal

After someone we love dies, grief is something we will always have with us.

The Memory Book: A Grief Journal for Children and Families is designed as a resource and a keepsake you can use to remember your loved one throughout the years and even to share new memories since they have passed away. It can be done alone, together as a family, or to help children in their grief. The pages are designed so you can choose the best way to cherish their memory, whether it's through writing, drawing, taping or gluing pictures, or a combination.

This journal isn't mean to be finished in a week, a month, or even a year—just like grief isn't something we "get over" in a short time. We will experience our first holidays without the person we've lost, anniversaries without them. We'll even have new milestones and memories without them. I hope this journal will also help you think of ways that your loved one can still be part of those moments.

The Memory Book is here to be a place to reflect and share memories and feelings. Browse the table of contents to find a section to help you choose a place to journal your memory. Prompts will lead you to think and remember about your loved one's life and how they have touched yours.

As you read the prompts, think about the ways to respond that feel best for you. You might want to respond in writing. Or you might prefer to draw a picture, or glue or tape a photograph or keepsake to the page. You might even want to go somewhere or do something, and document your experience. There's no wrong way to respond to the prompts in this book—only the way that feels right to you.

This journal is a companion to *The Memory Box: A Book About Grief*. That book recommends creating a box of memories as a way to process grief. That's another thing you can do as you fill in this book. Perhaps this journal will be a keepsake that will eventually go in your own memory box.

However you choose to use this book, I hope that it will be a comfort to you as you process your own feelings during the grieving process.

—Joanna Rowland

Always in our hearts.

In loving memory of

_____

Born:_____

Died:_____

The Story of You

Write the story of your loved one's life, using the details that matter most to you.

_____

_____

_____

_____

_____

_____

_____

_____

_____

_____

_____

_____

All about You

You will never be forgotten.

Places you lived: _____

_____

_____

_____

Jobs you had: _____

_____

_____

_____

_____

Favorite foods: _____

_____

_____

_____

_____

Favorite music, books, movies:

_____

_____

_____

_____

_____

_____

Hobbies: _____

_____

_____

_____

_____

_____

Your family and friends: _____

_____

_____

_____

All about You

Add drawings or photos of your loved one here.

I can never have another you. I miss you.

My first memory of you: _____

_____

_____

_____

_____

_____

You are special to me because _____

_____

_____

_____

_____

I miss you whenever I think about _____

_____

_____

_____

_____

Sometimes, I wonder what happens
to your love now that you're gone?
Did it die too?
Because I'm scared
I'll forget you.

I wonder: _____
_____
_____
_____
_____

I fear: _____
_____
_____
_____
_____

I hope: _____
_____
_____
_____

Sometimes, I wish I could give you a hug.

My favorite day with you was _____

_____

_____

_____

_____

_____

_____

_____

_____

_____

_____

_____

If I had
one more day
with you, I would . . .

_____

_____

_____

_____

_____

_____

_____

_____

_____

_____

_____

_____

_____

_____

I want to go
EVERYWHERE we visited.

We've been to _____

This place we've been is special because _____

_____

_____

_____

_____

We've been to _____

This place we've been is special because _____

_____

_____

_____

_____

We've been to _____
_____
_____

This place we've been
is special because ____
_____
_____
_____
_____

We've been to _____

This place we've been is special because _____
_____
_____
_____
_____

I want to go EVERYWHERE you've been.

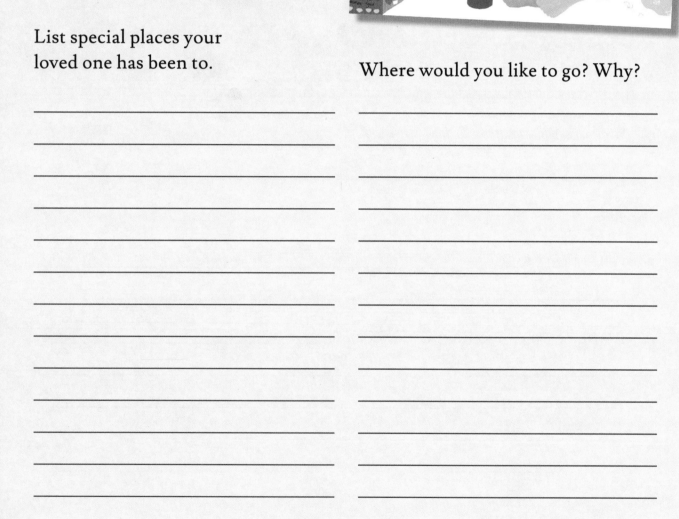

List special places your loved one has been to.

_____

_____

_____

_____

_____

_____

_____

_____

_____

_____

Where would you like to go? Why?

_____

_____

_____

_____

_____

_____

_____

_____

_____

_____

More special places

Draw or add photos of special places here.

Some days are good.
I laugh. I smile.

Today I was comforted by _____

_____

_____

_____

_____

_____

I smiled today when _____

_____

_____

_____

_____

_____

Other days, I wonder if I'll ever stop feeling sad you're gone.

Today was a bad day because _____
_____
_____

_____

_____

I feel sad, worried, or scared whenever
I think about _____
_____
_____
_____
_____
_____

But I always think of you.
SO MANY THINGS remind me of you.

Things that remind me of you

_____ _____

_____ _____

_____ _____

_____ _____

_____ _____

_____ _____

_____ _____

_____ _____

_____ _____

_____ _____

I thought of you today when _____

_____

_____

_____

_____

_____

_____

_____

_____

_____

_____

_____

The sound of _____
reminds me of _____
_____
_____
_____
_____
_____
_____
_____
_____
_____
_____
_____
_____
_____

When I see _____

it reminds me of _____

_____

_____

_____

_____

_____

_____

Looking at _____

brings back memories of _____

_____

_____

_____

_____

_____

_____

_____

_____

The smell of _____

reminds me of _____

_____

_____

_____

_____

_____

_____

The taste of _____

reminds me of _____

_____

_____

_____

_____

_____

_____

Holding _____

makes me think/feel _____

_____

_____

_____

_____

_____

_____

The feeling of _____

reminds me of _____

_____

_____

_____

_____

_____

_____

Today I'm asking everyone about their favorite memories of you.

Memory: _____

_____

_____

_____

_____

Told by _____

Memory: _____

_____

_____

_____

Told by _____

Memory: _____

_____

_____

_____

_____

Told by _____

Memory: _____

_____

_____

_____

_____

Told by _____

Memory: _____

_____

_____

_____

Told by _____

Memory: _____

_____

_____

_____

_____

Told by _____

Memory: _____

_____

_____

_____

_____

Told by _____

Memory: _____

_____

_____

_____

_____

Told by _____

Memory: _____

_____

_____

_____

_____

Told by _____

Memory: _____

_____

_____

_____

_____

Told by _____

Memory: _____

_____

_____

_____

_____

Told by _____

It helps me when I think about our special times. And it even helps to still do the things we'd planned to do together. You're still with me in my heart.

My favorite memories

I remember _____

_____

_____

_____

_____

I'll never forget _____

_____

_____

_____

_____

_____

One of my favorite memories is

_____

_____

_____

_____

_____

_____

_____

_____

_____

I'll never forget _____

_____

_____

_____

_____

_____

_____

One of my favorite memories is _____
_____
_____
_____
_____
_____

I remember _____
_____
_____
_____
_____

I'll never forget _____
_____
_____
_____
_____

One of my favorite memories is _____
_____
_____
_____
_____
_____
_____

I remember _____
_____
_____
_____
_____
_____

I'll never forget _____
_____
_____
_____
_____

Draw or add photographs or mementos of more memories here.

I will forever cherish our special traditions.

Did you have special traditions around the holidays, birthdays, a favorite meal, sports team, place? Use this section to write those down.

Holiday traditions: _____

_____

_____

_____

_____

_____

_____

_____

_____

_____

_____

_____

Birthday traditions: _____

_____

_____

_____

_____

_____

_____

_____

_____

Special outings and activities: _____

_____

_____

_____

_____

_____

_____

_____

_____

_____

No season will ever be the same without you here.

Spring memory: _____
_____
_____
_____
_____
_____
_____

Spring without you: _____
_____
_____
_____
_____
_____
_____

Summer memory: _____
_____
_____
_____
_____
_____
_____

Summer without you: _____
_____
_____
_____
_____
_____
_____
_____
_____

Fall memory: _____
_____
_____
_____
_____
_____

Fall without you: _____
_____
_____
_____
_____
_____
_____
_____
_____

Winter memory: _____

_____

_____

_____

_____

_____

Winter without you: _____

_____

_____

_____

_____

_____

_____

_____

Now I'm making new memories.

It can feel so hard to go on when our loved one is no longer with us. Especially when there are special events such as weddings, birthdays, holidays, and births. But it can be healing to write them down to our loved one. Write in this section about a new memory you wish you could share with them.

I wish you were here to see _____

_____

_____

_____

_____

_____

_____

_____

_____

_____

_____

_____

Today I _____

_____

_____

_____

_____

_____

_____

_____

_____

_____

_____

_____

_____

_____

_____

_____

_____

_____

I wish you were here for _____

_____

_____

_____

_____

_____

_____

_____

_____

_____

_____

_____

_____

_____

Something special happened today: _____

_____

_____

_____

_____

_____

_____

_____

_____

_____

_____

_____

_____

_____

I have so many things I'd like to say to you.

Write a letter to your loved one.

_____

_____

_____

_____

_____

_____

_____

_____

_____

_____

_____

I remember times with you.

Anniversaries such as birthdays and holidays can be difficult times.

Writing down your feelings on those days can be helpful. Is there something you can do to honor them on this day? Can you look at photo albums? Visit their grave? Go to a place you shared special memories? Gather people for a meal to share in their memory?

_____

_____

_____

_____

_____

_____

_____

_____

_____

_____

_____

I'm making a box
so I won't forget you.

A memory box can be something you create to hold
and share memories. This journal could be something
you keep inside the box.

What things would you put inside a memory box?
Look at other pages in this journal to give you more ideas.

_____

_____

_____

_____

_____

_____

_____

_____

_____

_____

More memories
I will hold in my heart.

Use these pages for memories, reflections, thoughts, and keepsakes.

_____

_____

_____

_____

_____

_____

_____

_____

_____

_____

_____

More memories

More memories

_____
_____
_____
_____
_____
_____
_____
_____
_____
_____
_____
_____
_____

More memories

More memories

More memories

More memories

More memories

I was afraid I would forget you.
But I won't.

You'll always be with me
no matter where I go.

Whenever I miss you
I'll think of you.

And I'll never forget.

We will carry you in our hearts by _____

_____

_____

_____

About the Author & Illustrator

 **JOANNA ROWLAND** grew up in Sacramento, California, where she still lives today with her husband and three children. She teaches kindergarten by day and writes picture books at night. In the summer, you'll find her at the pool coaching synchronizing swimming or cozying up with a book. She is the author of *The Memory Box: A Book about Grief.*

 **THEA BAKER** grew up in a country town in England. She is currently living in Australia and working internationally as a children's illustrator. Thea obtained her BA (Hons) Degree in illustration at the prestigious Falmouth University. Her dissertation was on the subject of grief in children's books.